POLITICALLY CORRECT
OLD TESTAMENT STORIES

POLITICALLY CORRECT OLD TESTAMENT STORIES

ROBERT MARTIN WALKER

ANDREWS AND McMEEL
A Universal Press Syndicate Company
Kansas City

Politically Correct Old Testament Stories
copyright © 1997 by Robert Martin Walker.
All rights reserved. Printed in the United States
of America. No part of this book may be used or
reproduced in any manner whatsoever except in the case of
reprints in the context of reviews. For information, write to
Andrews and McMeel, a Universal Press Syndicate Company,
4520 Main Street, Kansas City, Missouri 64111.

Library of Congress Cataloging-in-Publication Data

Walker, Robert Martin.
Politically correct Old Testament stories / Robert Martin.
p. cm.
ISBN 0-8362-3198-8
1. Bible stories. English—O.T. 2. Political correctness—Humor.
3. American wit and humor. 4. Humor—Religious aspects.
5. Bible. O.T.—Humor. I. Title.
BS550.2.W25 1997
221.9′505—dc21   96-48036
                                                     CIP

Attention: Schools and Businesses
Andrews and McMeel books are available at quantity
discounts with bulk purchase for educational,
business, or sales promotional use.
For information, please write to: Special Sales Department,
Andrews and McMeel, 4520 Main Street,
Kansas City, Missouri 64111.

For Wil, whose humor runs deep
and whose laughter rings true.

"Now Sarah said, 'God has brought laughter for me; everyone who hears will laugh with me.'"
(Genesis 21:6)

CONTENTS

CONTENTS

INTRODUCTION

HE STORIES OF THE Old Testament are filled with rich humor. Because they are a part of Holy Scripture, we often miss their amusing twists and turns. We allow the seriousness with which we approach Scripture to eclipse the laughter that lives and breathes in these wonderful tales.

Yet, Abraham laughed. Sarah laughed. I believe that the Lord must have laughed, too, at the silliness and foibles of the creatures who lived in Canaan many centuries ago. I'll bet the Lord is still laughing, at us and with us.

My intent in this book is to bring to life the humor laying dormant in the Old Testament. Political correctness is simply a lens through which we can see the hilarity hidden in these stories. Recasting them in politically correct terms not only shows the absurdity of our strained efforts to be tolerant and sensitive, it exposes the folly of imposing our values on the ancient cultures found in the Old Testament. My hope is, finally, that we can see ourselves in these tales—and enjoy a hearty laugh.

While I am not an Old Testament scholar, I have relied on scholars to deepen my understanding of these stories. One scholar deserves special mention. For the tales in Genesis, I am indebted to W.J.A. Power, whose book, *Once Upon a Time: A Humorous Re-telling of the Genesis Stories,* has provided much inspiration and insight.

I am also grateful to others who have played a role in bringing this book to fruition: my intensity-endowed agent, Denise Marcil; my humor-gifted editor, Kathy Viele; and my coequal spouse, Donna, whose laughter is the standard by which I measure what is funny.

THE BESTOWAL OF GENDER IDENTITIES

The Creation of Adam and Eve

Genesis 2:4b-25

FTER EARTH WAS first created, and before it was instilled with the proper ecological balance, there were no plants or crops. However, there was plenty of mud due to a single stream that bubbled up from the ground and watered it each evening.

As the Creator slogged through the mud one day, a Great Idea sprang from the Divine Mind. "I know just what Earth needs! Someone other than Myself to make this place a hospitable habitat for plants and nonhumyn animals."

The Creator bent down, scooped up a handful of mud, and started fashioning a clay creature. When the Creator was satisfied with the design, the Creator blew into the creature's nostrils. Miraculously, the creature became a living humyn person. This person, being made in the image of the Creator, was gender-neutral.

The Creator quickly realized that a humyn being couldn't live on a mud flat without vegetation. So the Creator planted a lush garden and called it Eden. In the middle of Eden, two trees were planted: the Tree of Life and the Tree of Moral Knowledge. The Creator also dug a river through Eden, in case irrigation became necessary.

The Creator placed the humyn person in the garden and gave it a title: Head Horticulturist. The Creator also gave the person a strong suggestion: "You may freely eat anything in the garden except from the Tree of Moral Knowledge and the Tree of Life. If you eat the fruit of these trees, you will surely become nonliving."

The person nodded its head in acknowledgment of the Creator's words. Of course, the person was very curious as to why the Tree of Moral Knowledge was so special.

Then the Creator said, "It is not good for a humyn person to be alone. I will make a companion for it." The Creator went to work creating birds, insects, and animals. After each species was created, the Creator would show it to the person to see whether it met its criteria for companionship. The person also named each creature.

First, the Creator brought a creature who had a long neck, two long legs, and was covered with feathers.

The person carefully examined it. "I'm calling this creature 'Ostrich.' Because it is cerebrally challenged, it definitely won't do as a companion."

Next, the Creator brought a small, eight-legged creature covered with fuzzy hair.

The person wrinkled its nose. "You've got to be kidding! I can't have a relationship with this . . . tarantula. I have a strong urge to squash it with a rock."

Then the Creator brought a four-legged creature covered with black fur to the person.

The person said, "You're getting closer. I could see a short-term relationship with this . . . Labrador Retriever. In the long run, however, I need a companion who speaks rather than barks."

The Creator paraded creature after creature past the person, and all were rejected as potential candidates for a long-term, meaningful relationship. Frustrated, the Creator tried a different approach.

The Creator caused the person to fall into a deep sleep and surgically removed a rib. The Creator took a whittling knife and sculpted a creature that looked very similar to the person and breathed life into it.

When the first person awoke, it saw the newly created person and was delighted.

"This is just what I'm looking for in a companion," the first person said. "But I have a vague feeling that something's not quite right."

"I, too, feel we're lacking something important," the second person agreed. "What could it be?"

The Creator then realized what had been omitted from these persons' anatomies and hurriedly put them both to sleep. Each person was given a different gender identity. One person was designated "male" and the other "female," each receiving the appropriate organs, body shape, and hormones. This was accomplished simultaneously so as to engender equality and partnership between the sexes.

When the First Man and First Womyn awoke they looked each other over with widening eyes and said, "Now we can see what we were missing! Let's be coequal partners." They ran off to frolic in the shade of the Tree of Moral Knowledge.

THE ORIGINAL *FAUX PAS*

The First Sin

Genesis 3:1–24

N THE GARDEN OF Eden lived a walking, talking reptile companion who was cleverness-gifted. One day, this snake engaged the First Womyn, who had taken the name "Eve," in conversation. The snake piqued Eve's interest by discussing the components of a healthful diet.

Steering the conversation to the topic of the two arboreal companions in the center of the garden, the snake said, "So, I hear that you're not welcome to partake of the trees in the garden. Shouldn't you eat of all the food groups?"

Eve replied, "You are mistaken, my reptilian friend. The Lord said that we could eat of every tree in the garden except for the Tree of Moral Knowledge and the Tree of Life. We can achieve a balanced diet without their fruit."

The snake asked, "What will happen if you ingest the fruit of those trees?"

Wanting to impress the snake, Eve said, "If we even *touch* either of these trees, we will become nonliving!"

The snake said in a mocking tone, "That's just an old spouse's tale. You won't become nonliving. God knows that if you eat of the Tree of Moral Knowledge you will become godlike because you'll be able to discern between good and evil."

Eve said, "I don't understand. What is the meaning of 'good' and 'evil'?"

The snake said, "They are the major components of moral knowledge. Those who possess such knowledge will become as wisdom-enhanced as the Creator."

Eve was now intensely curious about the Tree of Moral Knowledge. She walked over to it and looked at the lovely, waxy fruit hanging from its branches. Her salivary glands secreted at the thought of a bite of the luscious edible pulpy mass. She was also enticed by the thought of knowing good from evil, which, after talking to the snake, she felt was a major deficiency in her education.

She plucked a piece of fruit and took a bite. She closed her eyes and waited. She was still alive! Then, she gave the fruit to her male companion, who was called "Adam." Adam had followed her to the tree. Not wanting to seem courage-deprived, he boldly took a bite.

Suddenly, their eyes opened wider! They stared at each other in amazement, filled with the knowledge that they were . . . *nudists!*

Adam said, "Oh my gosh! We're unwitting participants in an alternative lifestyle! Think of the teasing our children will receive in school. And, without clothing, we're exposed to all kinds of dangers."

Eve, who was not as embarrassed to be naked, said, "Like what?"

Adam said, "Without clothing we are psychologically vulnerable and emotionally fragile."

Eve muttered, "I thought eating the fruit would make us wise. The snake was not truthful."

Adam didn't hear the womyn's comment because he was busy sewing fig leaves together to make a pair of briefs. Because he was not yet fixed in a male gender role, he sewed Eve a fig leaf bikini.

"This is scratchy," she complained after putting it on.

Before Adam could respond, they heard the sound of the Creator taking an evening walk in the garden. Knowing that they had committed a *faux pas*, they did what is natural to humyns who are guilt-gifted: they hid.

The Creator called out to Adam, "Where are you?" Of course, the Creator already knew what had happened, but wanted to teach the First Man and First Womyn a lesson.

Adam began to justify his untenable moral position: "I was hiding from you because I was bashful. You see, I was naked and . . ."

"Who told you that you were naked?" asked the Creator. When Adam was silent, the Creator got right to the point: "Have you eaten from the tree that I very strongly suggested you not eat from?"

Adam, realizing that he was in a sensitive situation, pointed to Eve. "If you hadn't created her, I wouldn't be in this moral mess. She made me eat. She said if I didn't, she would withhold conjugal privileges."

The Creator said to Eve, "What in the world have you done?"

Eve, stunned at Adam's untruthful comment, quickly decided to cover her posterior with something other than fig leaves. She pointed at the snake who was nearby. "The snake took advantage of my lack of moral experience and lured me into eating."

The Creator, annoyment-abled by all this blame-passing, didn't wait to hear the snake's excuse.

The Creator addressed the snake: "Because you have contributed to the delinquency of an adult, you will no longer be able to vocalize your opinions. Your speech will be limited to hissing noises.

Also, your freedom of movement will be diminished by an inability to walk. You will henceforth crawl on your belly and slither."

The snake thought to itself, *This isn't so bad.*

The Creator added, "And, one more thing . . . from now on wimmin will be hate-gifted toward you and your offspring. They'll try to stomp your head whenever they see you."

Next, Eve was addressed by the Creator. "Now that you possess moral knowledge, you know that nonmoral actions have logical and natural consequences. You and the First Male will be assigned gender roles. From now on, you'll have pain in childbirth."

Eve thought to herself, *How is this a logical and natural consequence of eating fruit?*

The Creator continued, "Also, you'll have less physical power than your male partner. This, of course, doesn't mean that your gender is in any way inferior to the male gender."

To Adam, the Creator said, "Because you listened to the First Womyn instead of to me, no more easy street for you. Your gender role will be to exploit the earth to grow food."

Adam thought, *Compared to Eve and the snake, I got off pretty easy.*

The Creator said, "There's one more consequence. All of you are being invited to leave this garden."

Adam fell down on the ground and exhibited preadult behavior by kicking and screaming. Eve began to cry. The snake hissed defiantly.

Adam and Eve looked pathetic, wearing wilting fig leaves and defeated expressions. The Creator became pity-enhanced toward the persons (but not the snake).

"I'll give you a positive consequence to counterbalance these negatives," the Creator said. "Even though you will have pain in childbirth and toil in work, I'll gift you with sexual pleasure. I know it's not much, but it's the best I can do on short notice."

Adam winked at Eve and said, "Let's take advantage of the Lord's positive consequence." Eve quickly replied, "I have a headache."

UNDERACHIEVING CAIN
AND OBEDIENCE-GIFTED ABEL

Cain and Abel

Genesis 4:1–16

FTER ADAM AND
Eve had been invited by the Lord to leave the
Garden of Eden, they decided to begin a family.
Adam believed that sexual intercourse between two
mutually consenting adults was morally justified.
Eve, a coequal partner in the relationship, subjected
herself to this form of sexual exploitation, reasoning, "It's the only way to perpetuate the humyn
species." In any case, they knew each other in the
biblical sense and was a male preadult was born.

They named their firstborn Cain. Adam commented, "I have produced a male heir with the help of the Lord." Eve, hoping to break the patriarchal cycle of progeny, said, "Let's try for a girl!" Thus, Abel, another male person, was born.

Adam and Eve raised Cain and Abel to each fulfill their individual potential in consistency with their inherent abilities. Adam said, "We should not impose our parental expectations on our preadults, lest they not mature into individuated adults." Eve agreed in a coequal way, "Yes. We should not oppress our preadults with a parentalist viewpoint."

Now Abel was specially abled in the field of animal spousery. He became a keeper of sheep and was careful to respect the sheeps' rights as nonhumyn animals. He fed them organically grown grains, was careful not to let them overgraze, and protected them from nonhumyn predators such as wolves (although he was careful not to harm or injure the wolves, realizing that they were only fulfilling their inherent carnivorous nature).

Cain, the chronologically advantaged son, was horticulturally abled. He became a grower of healthful crops and was an ovo-lacto vegetarian. He was also gifted with a special character trait; namely, he was motivationally challenged.

Being respectful of their birthparents, Cain and Abel wanted to participate in Adam and Eve's religious traditions. One of those traditions was to offer ritual sacrifices to the Lord.

Cain had an easy time deciding what to offer to the Lord on the day of sacrifice. Expending the least possible energy, he collected some fruits and vegetables he was about to throw on the compost pile. He knew that plants were nonsentient and, therefore, could not feel pain at being cut, plucked, or yanked out of the ground (although he had performed these actions with reverence for the position of plants in the food chain). So, he brought to the Lord an offering of rotting fruits, nuts, and vegetables—a kind of stale trail mix.

Abel, however, agonized over what he ought to offer the Lord. He knew that tradition called for cruelly murdering a one-year-old sheep and bringing to the Lord the nonhealthful fat portions. He couldn't understand why the Lord would want him to exploit nonhumyn animals in this way. But, because he was obedience-gifted he was able to overcome the oppression of guilt over animal murder and killed the very best sheep of his flock for an offering to the Lord.

Cain and Abel brought their respective gifts to the altar of the Lord. As they each stood by their offering, they heard the voice of the Lord addressing them from a cloud.

"Cain, even though I affirm your love of my creation and your care of the land, your offering does not please me. You know that I value the burned fat of animals over that of green vegetables. Vegetables stink when burned. Besides, I noticed that the fruit was rotten and the vegetables were wilted. You have underachieved." Cain hung his head in shame over having displeased the Lord, feeling marginalized by the Lord's comments.

Then the Lord spoke again, "Abel, your offering is pleasing to me. I love the smell of burning fat from murdered animals because it reminds me of bacon frying in the morning. I am also sensitive to the fact that you had to overcome a moral commitment to the rights of nonhumyn animals in order to be obedient to me." Abel was secretly pleased by this compliment, even though he felt that Cain had been treated unjustly by the Lord.

When the cloud of the Lord's presence departed, Cain yelled at Abel, "Animal exploiter! How dare you cruelly murder a powerless, sentient creature. I have a mind to gift you with some reverence for life with this rock I'm holding."

Abel, deeply hurt by Cain's verbal abuse, said repentently, "My horticulturally gifted sibling, you are correct in your evaluation of my moral character. I was temporarily feeling-impaired. I placed pleasing the Lord over my commitment to justice for non-humyn animals."

Upon hearing Abel's confession, a deep feeling of sensitivity to Abel's needs rose up in Cain's throat, almost choking him. He cried out, "My poor sibling! Fortunately for you I possess a forgiveness-enhanced character. Will you give up your exploitation of non-humyn animals and join me in growing organic foods?"

"Oh yes!" cried Abel with deep siblingly feeling.

In heartfelt gratitude Abel stepped toward Cain to embrace him. In doing so, he slipped on a banana peel Cain had carelessly dropped and hit his head on the sharp-edged rock that Cain had cast down. He was immediately rendered nonviable. Cain thought to himself as he walked away, *This is justice, for he shouldn't have murdered the sheep.*

The Lord appeared on the scene and sounded patience-challenged. "Where is your brother, Abel?" he asked.

Cain, believing that the Lord would think the story of Abel's accidental death to be an untruth, answered, "How should I know? Am I my sibling's codependent?"

The Lord then became anger-enhanced. "What have you done? Your brother's blood is crying out to me from the ground. From now on, you will be blessing-impoverished. No longer will the earth you till grow organically fertilized crops. You will be forced to use pesticides, herbicides, and fungicides. Soil erosion will plague you because you will not be allowed to rotate your crops. Finally, you will be invited to wander the earth and live off society's welfare."

Cain pleaded, "O Lord, please don't coerce me into an alternate lifestyle. If I wander from place to place living off social welfare, I might be terminally inconvenienced!"

The Lord became compassion-abled toward Cain. "Don't worry. I'll put a mark on you so that those rendered compassion-challenged by social conditioning will not murder you. In fact, I'll allow you to do organic farming as long as you do it some where else."

So Cain went to the land of Nod, east of Eden, and organized an organically grown food cooperative. He omitted bananas from his future offerings to the Lord.

NOAH AND THE GENDER-EQUALIZED FLOTATION DEVICE

Noah and the Ark

Genesis 6–9

FTER SEVERAL GEN-
erations of fruitfully multiplying, the earth increased
in humyn population density. Unfortunately, as the
quantity of humyns grew, their ethical quality diminished. The Lord performed a moral evaluation
of the behavior of humynkind and was not pleased.

The Lord commented, "I must put an end to this
mess I created. Humyns are filled with violence toward each other as well as toward botanical companions and nonhumyn animals. Insensitivity is

rampant. It's time to close this chapter of hystory and start over."

There was one exception to the Lord's negative evaluation: Noah. Noah was a paragon of sensitivity and tolerance. He wouldn't harm any sentient beings. Noah was even respectful of the rights of nonsentient nonliving entities such as rocks and driftwood. A coequal partner with Ms. Noah, he was also an affirming parent to their offspring. For these reasons, the Lord decided to spare Noah's nuclear family from the moral cleansing of the earth.

One day, while Noah was busy hugging a cypress tree, the Lord spoke to him. "Noah. I've decided to wipe every living thing off the face of the earth, except for you and your family. It's going to rain for forty days and nights. Therefore, you need to build a size-enhanced flotation device."

Noah, astonished at being addressed by the Lord, said, "You mean an ark?"

The Lord said, "Yes. Build it from cypress wood and make it waterproof. It needs to be large enough to carry a substantial cargo."

Noah, reeling from the shock of hearing that his beloved cypress trees would be murdered, asked, "Lord, don't you think this flood idea is a little harsh?"

The Lord thundered, "I've given everyone second, third, and fourth chances to shape up. They just aren't making any progress."

"But why do you have to destroy all the innocent nonhumyn animals and botanical companions, especially the cypress trees?" asked Noah.

"That's why you're building such a large flotation device. You'll be carrying the male and female of each species," said the Lord.

Satisfied with the Lord's answer, Noah set out to build an ark. Realizing that he couldn't build it alone, he called a meeting of his biological family. The meeting was chaired by Ms. Noah.

"This family meeting will come to order," Ms. Noah said, clapping her hands together. "Noah, you may have the floor."

Noah stood up so that everyone could hear. "I've been asked by the Lord to build a huge boat and I would appreciate the assistance of every member of this family."

Seth, the most chronologically gifted child, raised his hand. Ms. Noah said, "The chair recognizes Seth."

Seth said, "Could you enlighten us as to the reason for building a boat here in the desert? There isn't a body of navigable water for miles!" There were murmurs of approval from Seth's siblings.

Noah said, "The Lord says it's going to rain for forty days. Whatever's not on the ark will be drowned."

Ham, another male offspring, raised his hand and was recognized. "Even if what you say is true, what will the neighbors think about building an ark in our front yard? We'll be the laughingstock of Canaan!"

Noah said, "There's more. We have to find the male and female of every species to bring onto the ark. This ark is to be inclusive and gender-balanced."

Suddenly, everyone was shouting questions at Noah. The volume increased until Ms. Noah clapped her hands together several times.

"Order! Order! Let us be respectful of one another's selfhood!" Ms. Noah said. "Please speak one at a time."

Japheth raised his hand. "How are we going to identify both genders of every species? For instance, how can we tell the difference between a male and female sand crab? Or, what about snakes and other species without visible sex organs?!"

Several of the female preadults giggled when Japheth said "sex organs." Ms. Noah gave them a stern stare and they were silent.

Noah said, "We'll just do the best we can. The Lord knows that we're not botanists or zoologists."

Ms. Noah said, "There is a motion on the floor by Noah to build an ark and fill it with both sexes from every species. All in favor, say 'aye.' "

There were a few unenthusiastic "ayes."

Ms. Noah said, "All opposed signify by saying 'nay.' "

There were several adamant "nays."

Ms. Noah, wanting to be supportive of her spouse, said, "The motion has passed."

Chaos erupted again. Family members were yelling at each other and violating each other's personal space. Noah walked away, wondering why the Lord wanted to spare his and Ms. Noah's nuclear family from the flood.

The building of the ark began. The neighbors objected strenuously to such a large, unsightly structure being built in a residential area. The NIMBYs brought a petition to the Canaan Planning and Zoning Commission to halt the project. However, by the time of the P&Z's next monthly meeting, the rains had started.

Recruiting both genders of every species proved to be challenging, just as Japheth had anticipated. The Noah family members adopted a "don't ask, can't tell" gender policy, settling for catching two specimens of the same species who looked different. It was difficult to find volunteers to capture carnivores like lions and tigers.

Finally, the ark was loaded and ready to go. Noah waved good-bye to his neighbors, who were shouting taunts and laughing uproariously. They had dubbed the ark *Noah's Folly*. Their laughter abruptly stopped when a booming thunderstorm erupted and hail pelted them.

It precipitated and precipitated. The water rose higher and higher. Soon the ark was floating and only the mountaintops were above water. Humyns scrambled to these high places and began fighting each other for the shrinking land. Finally, everything was underwater.

Life on the ark was . . . challenging. Noah had to make sure that predators like lions and tigers were separated from their prey of antelope and zebras. Feeding all the nonhumyn animals aboard was a monumental task. Much of the day had to be spent in waste removal; the elephants alone generated several hundred pounds of waste. As the fortieth day of rain approached, the ark had become so odor-enhanced that the Noah family had to wrap cloths around their nasal regions.

Finally, the rain stopped. Noah sent out a raven and a dove to see if they could find dry land. They returned exhausted. After a few more days, Noah sent out the dove again and it returned with an olive branch. The flood was over!

Noah landed the ark and trudged through the mud. He built an altar. Because there was no dry wood, he dismantled pieces of the ark and started a fire. Then, Noah took several ritually clean non-humyn animals and birds and murdered them, according to his religious tradition. He placed them on the fire and the smell of burning animal flesh wafted up to the Lord. Thus Noah inadvertently caused these species to become extinct.

The Lord was very pleased with Noah's sacrifice and said, "Noah, I've made an important decision. Never again will I perform a moral cleansing of the earth. It's too messy. I am going to make a contract with you and your descendants to not flood the earth again, no matter how morally deficient humyns become. To let you know how serious I am about this, I'll put a rainbow in the sky whenever it rains. This way, I won't forget to make the rain stop. Now, go and repopulate the earth."

Noah did as the Lord suggested. He lived to become very chronologically advanced. However, he was filled with remorseful feelings over murdering the cypress trees for the ark. To compensate, he planted an arboretum and tended it until he became nonliving.

ABRAHAM AND SARAH: FERTILITY-CHALLENGED

The Birth of Isaac

Genesis 12–18:15

HERE ONCE LIVED a person named Abraham, a male of ordinary ability. His coequal partner in marriage, Sarah, was also ordinary in every way except one: She had not yet become a birthmother to offspring. In ancient times, a child-deprived couple was considered inferior to a child-gifted couple. Thus, Abraham and Sarah became survivors of infertility.

Like other ancient people, Sarah and Abraham believed in Divine intervention. They prayed to the

Lord that their biological deficiency be corrected so they could parent an offspring.

The Lord heard their prayers and spoke to Abraham in a vision one night. The fact that Abraham was the one addressed by the Lord should not be construed as a nonaffirmation of Sarah. It just happened that Abraham fell asleep first that night.

In the vision, the Lord said, "Abraham, do not be phobic. You and Sarah will become the founders of a great nation."

Abraham replied, "O Lord, how can this be? Are you not aware that Sarah and I have no offspring? We've tried everything we can think of to become fetus-gifted. We've exhausted all the medical options. We're now making love upside down—"

"I don't need to know the details," the Lord interrupted. "Come outside and look up at the sky."

Abraham said, "It's very lovely, but what does this have to do with having a child?"

The Lord said, "You see how many stars there are? That's how many descendants you and Sarah will have."

When Abraham woke up, he told Sarah about his dream.

Sarah said, "Is that all? Didn't the Lord give you any specific instructions for conceiving?"

Abraham replied, "No, but I think it's pretty clear that the Lord is going to do *something*."

However, Sarah and Abraham continued to be fertility-challenged. Ten years passed. Needless to say, Sarah's biological clock was nearing midnight.

Sarah had a domestic manager, Hagar, who helped out with the household chores. Sarah, being open-minded for a womyn in a patriarchal society, decided to recruit Hagar as a surrogate mother. Hagar was willing to enter into such a contract. Abraham was open to this idea, both because he wanted a child and because Hagar was fifty years younger than Sarah. Since fertility technology had not advanced to the stage of *in vitro* fertilization, Abraham and Hagar practiced *in Hagar* fertilization.

Within a few months, it was clear that Hagar was pregnant. Even though Sarah had conceived this arrangement, she began to suffer from womb envy.

To make matters less good, Hagar adopted a superior attitude toward Sarah. Sarah consulted with Abraham about what should be done with this conceit-enhanced surrogate. Abraham, not wanting to become involved in this sensitive issue for obvious reasons, delegated authority to Sarah. "Do whatever you think best," he said.

Sarah proceeded to verbally harass Hagar. When she could stand it no longer, Hagar resigned her position and ran away. Abraham was eighty-six years old when his and Hagar's offspring, Ishmael, was later born.

When Abraham was ninety-nine years old, the Lord approached him a second time in a vision.

The Lord said, "I'm going to make a long-term agreement with you. You and Sarah will be the ancestors of an exceedingly populous nation. From your offspring will come sovereigns of both sexes. And I will give the land of Canaan to you and your offspring. I will be their Sovereign and they will be my loyalists."

Abraham did what any thinking person would do after hearing such a fantastic promise: He fell on his face and laughed. He laughed so hard he could hardly catch his breath. Finally, he was able to speak.

"Lord, that's a good one. I just love Divine comedy."

The Lord said, "I'm serious."

Abraham wasn't laughing as he said, "Can a child be born to a geriatric couple? In case you haven't noticed, I'm pushing one hundred and Sarah's over ninety. The sand in our biological hourglass ran out years ago. Why don't we just make Hagar's and my offspring, Ishmael, the ancestor of this nation?"

The Lord said, "No, I have other plans for Ishmael. You and Sarah will have a male offspring and you will name him Isaac. This will occur within the next year."

Abraham said, "But Isaac means 'laughter.' That's a tough name to saddle a kid with. He'll be the butt of every joke with a name like that."

But the Lord ignored Abraham, having already departed.

A few months later, Abraham was taking a nap in his tent in a grove of oak trees at a place called Mamre. He was awakened by three strangers standing before him. Abraham, a consummate host, invited them to supper. When they were comfortably seated in the shade, he brought them water to wash their feet and then excused himself.

Abraham became a whirlwind of activity. He requested that Sarah make some of her excellent granola cakes. He then ran to his herd, murdered a choice bovine companion, and asked an enslaved person to scorch its carcass. In a short time, he brought the cakes and scorched flesh to the strangers, along with some stolen nonhumyn animal products. To demonstrate his politeness, he attended them while they ate.

After they finished, one of the strangers said, "I will return to you in nine months. By that time, you and Sarah will have a male offspring."

Sarah, being gifted with curiosity, was hiding a short distance away, listening to the conversation. This time, it was Sarah's turn to laugh. She laughed so hard that she pulled a muscle in her abdomen. Even then she couldn't stop.

"What's so funny?" the stranger asked.

"Don't you get it?" Sarah giggled. "I've been

postmenopausal for decades and Abe—well, Abe's spirit is willing but the flesh is a little weak. We're just not reproductively empowered."

As Sarah finished her discourse, the strangers disappeared. In their place stood the Lord.

The Lord said, "I'm becoming annoyed with you two. Every time I make a serious promise, one of you bursts into laughter. This isn't a comedy routine. I'm trying to enable you to become parents of a great nation. Would you like it if I were laughter-enriched at your expense?"

Sarah and Abraham were much abashed. Sarah was so embarrassed that she said, "I wasn't laughing. I just had something caught in my throat and was performing the Heimlich maneuver on myself."

Unamused, the Lord said, "I know laughter when I hear it. Now, am I going to get some cooperation from you two?"

Sarah and Abraham shook their heads yes.

The Lord said, "Okay. Now get into that tent and don't tell me you have headaches!"

Sarah and Abraham went into the tent and closed the flap. After a few minutes, four eyes peered out of the tent to make sure the Lord had left. Clear strains of hilarity again echoed among the oaks of Mamre and the tent began to shake. Nine months later they were gifted with the child of their laughter, Isaac.

JOSEPH THE
FLAMBOYANT EGOIST

Joseph and the Coat of Many Colors
Genesis 37

FTER HIS FATHER, Isaac, died, Jacob (a.k.a. Israel) settled in the land of Canaan. He then established a multinuclear family. In those unenlightened days, polygamy wasn't considered a moral taboo. Jacob had four spouses, who eventually bore him twelve male offspring. Because feminism was still a few millennia in the future, Jacob's spouses willingly submitted to this form of patriarchal oppression. They lived together in one large blended family sharing coequally in the marital rights and responsibilities. This arrangement was the precursor of our modern-day job sharing.

Of the twelve male offspring, Joseph was the least oldest. More important, he was Jacob's favorite. Because Jacob loved Joseph in an unhealthy, inequitable, and codependent manner, he granted his every wish. If Joseph demanded a toy, Jacob had one of his other sons make it. If Joseph whined for the scorched carcass of a nonhumyn animal, Jacob commanded a son to murder the voiceless victim and barbecue its flesh. Because of this overindulgence, Joseph became conceit-enhanced. Consequently, Joseph's siblings were gifted with animosity toward him.

One day, Joseph decided to test the limits of his father's indulgence. He demanded an expensive colorful tunic, the kind of garment females wore on special occasions like festivals. This request caused Jacob much anxiety over Joseph's sexual orientation. However, because he desired to please his son and would love and accept him even if he embraced an alternative lifestyle, Jacob asked one of his spouses to make such a garment. Leah, Joseph's birthmother, having no clue that she was making the tunic for a male, used elaborate lace and gold brocade.

When Jacob presented his son with this colorful tunic, Joseph was ecstatic. Much to his father's embarrassment, he paraded around the house wearing it. When the rest of the blended family came home at the end of the workday, they were astonished at Joseph's garment and stunned that he would wear such a tunic. Not wanting to be seen as judgmental, they said nothing.

Joseph wore his colorful tunic everywhere: to meals, to work in the fields, and even to bed. Perhaps the tunic had something to do with the nocturnal visions Joseph began experiencing.

One day, Joseph shared one of his dreams with his siblings. "We were all in the field, exploiting Mother Earth, binding sheaves. Suddenly, my sheaf stood up and your sheaves gathered round it. Then, your sheaves bowed down to mine," he said.

Joseph's siblings didn't need a Freudian analyst to figure out what the dream meant. They said to Joseph, "What kind of phallocentric imagery is this? Who do you think you are? Joseph, Queen of the

Desert?" Their negative feelings toward Joseph were enhanced by the dream.

Oblivious to their intensely negative reaction to his first dream, Joseph enthusiastically shared another. "My second dream is even better! The Sun, the Moon, and eleven stars were bowing down to me." Joseph beamed with satisfaction after sharing this dream experience.

Jacob happened to be listening and was more than a little dismay-gifted. He asked, "What kind of nocturnal nonsense is this? Do you want your entire blended family, including your birthparents, to worship you?"

Joseph didn't answer and strutted away in his color-enhanced tunic like a member of the power elite.

Several days later, Joseph's eleven male siblings had taken the sheep to pasture several miles away, near Shechem. Jacob sent Joseph, who was leisurely picking the lint off his colorful tunic, to find out how things were going and bring back a report. Joseph, being motivationally deficient, was loathe to go. However, he couldn't engage his father's guilt feelings enough to escape this assignment.

Joseph soon became geographically dislocated and sought directional guidance from a seller of stolen nonhumyn animal products, who pointed Joseph in the right direction.

When his siblings saw him coming in the distance, they plotted to render him nonliving.

One of them said, "Here comes the nocturnal egoist. Let's terminally inconvenience him and throw his corpse in a pit! We'll tell our father that an untamed nonhumyn animal made a meal of him. Then he can dream eternally!"

But Rueben had moral misgivings over his siblings' plan. He offered an alternative course of action. "Let's not render him nonliving. Let's just toss him into the pit alive. He'll expire from benign neglect and our consciences will be clear." Rueben said this because he intended to rescue Joseph later.

Rueben's motion was seconded and passed by a vote of nine to one, with one abstention. When Joseph arrived, they person-handled him and relieved him of his colorful garment. They threw him into a nearby pit that had been created by well-diggers, and sat down to take nourishment.

At first, Joseph was so stunned he was speech-deprived. Once he realized that he was a survivor of sibling abuse, he began to wail, "Get me out! This practical joke was funny at first, but I'm not laughing now."

One of his siblings, Judah, verbally abused him, saying, "Why don't you dream your way out!"

Once they finished consuming a healthful lunch, Rueben went off to tend the sheep. A short time later, a caravan of Ishmaelites from Gilead riding hump-endowed animal companions drew near. Several of the offspring of Jacob recoiled at this exploitation of the camels, but, seeing the large swords worn by the Ishmaelites, decided it wasn't the appropriate time to be advocates for the camels' rights.

Judah had an epiphany. He said to his siblings, "I've done a cost-benefit analysis of this situation. Rather than letting Joseph die, let's exploit him for financial gain." This motion passed ten to zero

(Rueben was absent). So they helped Joseph out of the pit and sold him for twenty pieces of silver to the caravan, which promptly left for Egypt.

Judah devised a coverup of this escapade. They murdered a goat companion and dipped Joseph's tunic in its blood. Then they took it to Jacob and said, "Father, look what we found on our way home. It looks like Joseph's."

At first, Jacob was pleased, supposing that Joseph had abandoned his flamboyant manner of dressing. Then, he saw the blood and cried out, "An untamed nonhumyn animal must have feasted on my beloved Joseph!" He paused for a moment and added, "One thing bothers me. If he was torn apart by a nonhumyn animal, why isn't his tunic ripped?"

Thinking quickly, Judah replied, "Father, you know how protective Joseph was of his tunic. He must have taken it off so that it wouldn't be torn." All of Judah's siblings exhaled in relief when Jacob accepted this untruth.

Jacob entered into a mourning ritual that involved tearing his clothes and wearing an undergarment made of sackcloth, which was most unpleasant. His male and female offspring tried to comfort him, but he refused to be consoled.

Meanwhile, the Ishmaelites arrived in Egypt and sold Joseph to Potiphar, the captain of the Pharaoh's guard. Potiphar's spouse, being taken with Joseph, tried to induce him into a nonmonogamous relationship with her. When he refused, she made him a guest of the Egyptian penal system. Eventually, Joseph was able to use his dream-giftedness to get out of jail and rise into the Egyptian power elite. Then he had a tailor make him an even more outrageous tunic which he wore proudly.

MOSES AND THE FLAMING
BOTANICAL COMPANION

Moses and the Burning Bush

Exodus 3–4

FTER PERSON-
slaughtering an Egyptian who was physically abus-
ing an enslaved Hebrew, Moses became a refugee
from the legal authorities. He fled Egypt and settled in the land of Midian with a spouse named
Zipporah. They parented a male preadult and called
him Gershom, which means "alien," because he was
an undocumented worker in Midian.

Moses became a companion of sheep. One day,
he took the sheep to a high pasture on Mount Sinai
in search of fresh grass. As he watched the grazing

flock, he saw something unusual in his peripheral vision. A botanical companion was on fire. He ran toward the bush in an attempt to save it, but stopped several feet away. Strangely, the bush wasn't consumed by the flame. Even a prescientific person like Moses understood this was extraordinary.

Then something even more unusual happened. The botanical companion called out, "Moses, Moses."

Moses replied, "What's going on here?" He started walking toward the bush.

The bush said, "Stop! Take off your sandals, for you are in a biome containing rare lichen and moss!"

Moses did as the voice suggested.

The voice continued, "I am the Lord, the God of your foreparents Sarah and Abraham, Rebecca and Isaac, Leah and Jacob."

Moses turned away from the flaming botanical companion, for he had assimilated the belief of his religious tradition that to look upon God was to become nonliving.

Then the voice said, "I have seen the unjust suffering of my people who are abused as enslaved persons by the Egyptians. I am going to liberate them and bring them to a land flowing with products from bovine companions and bees."

Moses thought to himself, *I hope this doesn't involve my participation.*

The Lord continued, "I won't tolerate the oppression or marginalization of the Hebrew culture. Therefore, I am sending you to Pharaoh to emancipate the Israelites from Egyptian imperialism."

Moses, trying to stall the Lord until he could think of a good excuse to get out of this assignment, said, "If I go to my coequal Israelites and say, 'The God of my foreparents has sent me,' and they ask me, 'What is this God's name?' what do I say?"

The Lord said, "Tell them 'I am who I am' has sent you."

Moses' voice rose an octave as he said, "What kind of name is 'I am who I am'? It sounds more like a riddle than a name for a Divine Being. If I tell them this, they'll laugh me right back across the Nile!"

The Lord said, "Trust Me, they won't laugh. Assemble all the members of the Israelite power structure and tell them I'm going to lead them out of slavery into self-determination. Then, go to Pharaoh and tell him that you want to take all the Israelites on a three-day journey to a place in the wilderness to offer sacrifices to Me."

Moses said, "Do you really believe Pharaoh is going to let a million enslaved persons go just because I ask him? This doesn't sound like a workable plan."

The Lord said, "Do you think I'm foresight-impaired? I know that Pharaoh isn't going to ruin the Egyptian economy by allowing a low-cost source of labor to walk away. He won't let you go . . . *unless* he perceives the negative consequences of your staying. Here's phase two of my plan: I'll give you some impressive tricks to perform that will convince him that you're my spokesperson."

Moses, now curious, asked, "Like what?"

The Lord said, "What are you holding?"

Moses said, "A staff."

The Lord said, "Throw it down."

"Won't that hurt the lichen and moss?" Moses asked.

"Just do it," the voice from the bush strongly suggested.

Moses threw down the staff and immediately began hopping from one foot to the other because the staff had become a slithering snake!

The Lord said, "Now, pick it up."

Moses said, "I'm phobic of scaly reptiles." But Moses was more phobia-enriched toward the Lord than by the snake and did as the Lord said. When he grasped its tail, it became a staff again.

Moses said, "Wow! What other tricks do you have for me?"

The Lord said, "Put your hand inside your cloak and take it out again."

Moses did this and to his astonishment, the hand was covered with leprosy, a highly contagious skin disease. Moses wasn't liking this trick at all.

"Put your hand back inside your cloak and pull it out again," the Lord said.

Moses was very reluctant to do this for fear that the leprosy would spread to his upper thoracic region. But he conquered his phobia and did as the

Lord said. His hand was restored to normal! Moses now liked this trick much better.

Moses said, "These are really fine tricks, Lord. But what if they still won't believe that you are Sovereign over all creation and let the persons of Israel go?"

The Lord said, "Okay. If they're not impressed by the snake and hand tricks, take some water from the Nile and pour it on the ground. When it hits the ground it will become blood."

Moses thought, *This trick isn't as impressive as the first two*, but didn't dare share this thought.

Then Moses began to feel acutely insecure in his oracular abilities. He said, "My Lord. I've never been specially abled in the area of speaking. I'm definitely not gifted at making extemporaneous speeches. I have a tendency to stammer when I am nervous, which is often. But the biggest reason I can't be your spokesperson is that I speak Hebonics, which the Egyptians can't understand without bilingual education."

The Lord said firmly, "Who do you think created mortals and their voice boxes? Now go and I will whisper your lines to you when you confront Pharaoh with your demands."

Moses dropped to his knees and engaged in power-begging, "O Lord, *please* send someone else. Pharaoh is so big and powerful and is a human rights violator. Even with the tricks you've given me, I don't think he'll change his mind. He is stubbornness-gifted. And, please remember, I'm wanted for personslaughter in Egypt."

The Lord became mercy-enhanced toward Moses. "I'll tell you what I'll do. I'll send your chronologically advantaged male sibling, Aaron, to accompany you. He is accomplished in oration. He will be your spokesperson. Now, pick up your staff and head for Egypt."

Because Moses was challenged at quick thinking, he couldn't come up with any more excuses for not doing what the Lord suggested. He reluctantly headed toward Egypt, vowing to ignore all flammable botanical companions in the future.

THE TEN SUGGESTIONS

The Ten Commandments

Exodus 19:16–20:21

FTER WANDERING
in the wilderness for several months like a geographically dislocated sheep (even in ancient times
males were reluctant to seek directional guidance),
Moses finally led the persons of Israel to Mount
Sinai. There they set up a camp in balance with the
delicate desert ecosystem.

Moses went up to the mountaintop to converse
with the Lord, just as he had done the time he en-
countered the flammable botanical companion. In

those unenlightened times, persons believed that conversations with Divine Beings were possible. However, there were some faith-impaired persons among the Israelites who doubted that Moses really conversed with the Lord. To teach these naysayers a lesson, the Lord invited Moses to gather the people at the base of the mountain where they would witness an impressive display of Divine pyrotechnics.

The Lord also spoke a warning to Moses, "Don't allow anyone to come up the mountain, or to touch it, or they will become nonviable."

Moses replied, "But, technically, their feet will be touching the mountain."

"Don't be such a literalist," the Lord thundered.

Moses, being obedience-gifted, did everything the Lord suggested. To purify themselves for the Lord's revelation, Moses had every person wash his or her clothes. They also refrained from sexual relations for three days, which was very difficult for those who were libido-enhanced.

On the third day, Moses gathered the persons of Israel into an assembly. The top of the mountain was enshrouded with a thick cloud from which thunder and lightning issued forth. Everyone was very impressed.

Then a trumpet blast came from the cloud, the signal for Moses to lead the Israelites to the foot of the mountain. There was much soul-searching during the walk to the mountain among those who had been skepticism-enhanced about Moses' private audiences with the Lord.

Once they were gathered at the base of the mountain, a deep, resonant voice not unlike that of James Earl Jones came forth from the cloud.

"I have chosen to make this covenant with you: I will be your God; you will be my people. Now it's time for you to learn what it means to be my people. I'm giving you ten commandments to follow. Keep them and you will live," the voice rumbled.

Moses raised his hand, "Lord, forgive me for interrupting. But don't you think 'commandment' is a little too coercive? This might offend some of the persons of Israel who don't believe in moral absolutes. Couldn't we call them 'suggestions'? This would allow each person to accept them in a way consistent with his or her own value system."

For several seconds there was silence. Then a bolt of lightning struck near Moses' feet, accompanied by a clap of thunder. Everyone jumped, and the aroma of ozone filled their nostrils.

"I don't care what you call them, as long as you obey them!" the voice thundered.

Moses raised his hand again. "I don't mean to be a pest, Lord. But 'obey' is a pretty oppressive word . . ."

A bolt of lightning struck so close to Moses' feet that he danced as if his toes were on fire. Moses interpreted this as a suggestion that he ought to be silent.

Now that everyone's attention had been captured, the voice from the cloud again became audible.

"Remember that I am the Lord who brought you out of Egypt where you were enslaved persons. Therefore, you must worship only Me."

One person of Israel whispered to a friend, "That's pretty egotistical, isn't it?" A bolt of lightning immediately rendered this person nonliving.

"Any other comments?" asked the Lord. There was silence. "Good. Secondly, do not make any idols or worship them. This includes persons in the entertainment arts, as well as little clay figurines and so on. I am jealousy-endowed and am not inclined to play second lute in the choir."

A few persons of Israel were puzzled by this last metaphor, but said nothing for fear of being gifted with a lightning bolt.

"Next, do not misuse my name," said the Lord.

Moses timidly raised his hand. "Lord, could you give us an example of what you mean?" He closed his eyes, waiting for lightning to strike. It didn't.

"Of course I can. After all, I *am* God. Try not to speak my name loudly when you strike your thumb with a hammer or when a she-goat has eaten your best tunic.

"Next, do not work on the Sabbath. That's the day I am leisure-inclined and you should be the same."

There were murmurs of approval from the crowd at this fourth suggestion. There were also some patience-challenged stares toward Moses, who hadn't given the Israelites a day off since they left Egypt.

The Lord said, "Oh, I forgot to add that you should spend the Sabbath worshiping Me." The approving murmurs ceased.

"Next, be honor-inclined toward your birthparents."

The parents in the throng were pleasure-abled with this suggestion. However, the preadults were enthusiasm-challenged, especially those who were pubescent.

"Sixthly, do not murder. This goes for botanical companions, nonhumyn animals, and humyns."

Many persons thought, *What are we supposed to eat?* But no person said anything, remembering the Lord's accuracy with lightning.

"Next, be monogamous."

Several of the male persons of Israel looked down at their sandals as their spouses glared at them.

"Eighthly, do not coopt anything for personal use that is not yours.

"Ninthly, do not speak untruths."

Several persons of Israel thought, *This is going to*

be tough. But no person dared to share such thoughts aloud.

"And, lastly, do not be desire-inclined toward anything that belongs to other persons, including their dwellings, spouses, male or female enslaved persons, or ox or donkey, or any other nonhumyn animal."

After the voice from the cloud said "animal" there was immediately thunder, lightning, a seismic event, and other cataclysmic occurrences. The persons of Israel, including Moses, trembled with fear.

Then there was awe-inspiring silence. No person wanted to be the first to move. After several motionless minutes Moses' sibling, Aaron, nudged Moses with his pointy elbow and whispered, "Maybe you should ask the Lord to prioritize these suggestions. Doing them all would require significant lifestyle changes."

Moses broke the silence with a wavering voice, "Lord, is there anything else?"

"Are you mathematically challenged?" asked the Lord. "Ten commandments just about covers it all. Now go back and do what I told you."

Moses and the persons of Israel gave their best efforts to following the ten suggestions, but often fell short of total compliance. Fortunately, the Lord was forgiveness-inclined.

TESTOSTERONE-GIFTED
SAMSON

Samson and Delilah

Judges 14–16

NCE THERE LIVED
a judge of Israel whose name was Samson. Samson's
birthmother, like her foremother, Sarah, was chronologically advanced when he was born. She was so
grateful to have a child, she dedicated him to the
Lord. This is how Samson became a Nazarite. Nazarites lived an extremely healthful lifestyle. They did
not contaminate their bodies with fat-laden meats
such as pork, or drink alcohol of any kind. In those
days the medicinal benefits of drinking wine in mod-

eration were not understood. Another Nazarite vow was that no razor could touch their cranial hair.

From the time he reached puberty, it was clear that Samson was testosterone-gifted. He performed many feats of masculine aggression. When a young lion attempted to be a companion to Samson, he ripped the lion apart. This greatly upset members of the Society for the Protection of Carnivores. So active were his hormones that, one day when he saw a Philistine woman endowed with great physical beauty, he demanded that his birthparents arrange for her to become his spouse. His domestic incarceration to a Philistine was noteworthy as the Philistines were oppressors of the Israelites.

Because of a minor matter of Samson murdering thirty Philistines for their tunics to pay off a gambling debt, Samson's spouse was given to his best man. When Samson discovered this, his optimistic outlook on life was challenged. He felt it was exploitative to treat wimmin as possessions rather than as coequal partners. In a somewhat extreme response, Samson murdered a thousand Philistines with the jawbone of an ass. He soon became very unpopular with the Philistines. However, so great was Samson's strength that nobody was willing to confront him with his character flaws.

It wasn't long before Samson fell in love again. This time, it was with a beauty-endowed Philistine named Delilah. Delilah had some character flaws of her own. As a survivor of an economically deprived family, she suffered from materialism. When the members of the Philistine power elite offered Delilah several thousand pieces of silver to discover the secret of Samson's strength, she agreed in a Jericho minute.

One evening Delilah stroked Samson's ego, taking advantage of his testosterone-enhanced condition. "Oh, Samson. You're so size-gifted, strength-gifted, and testosterone-gifted. I'd like to tie you up so you couldn't get loose."

Samson asked, "Why?"

Delilah answered coyly, "You'll see."

Samson said quickly, "If you tie me up with seven fresh bowstrings that haven't dried out, I couldn't escape."

Samson helped Delilah find the bowstrings and

even assisted her in tying some of the more difficult knots. When he was bound, Delilah decided to test the bowstring hypothesis.

"The Philistines are coming, Samson!"

Samson leapt up and the bowstrings stretched like rubber bands and snapped.

Delilah put on a pouting act, which wasn't difficult since she was in danger of not getting the silver pieces.

She whined, "Samson, you have lowered my self-esteem by telling me an untruth. You're going to be sleeping on the guest pallet if you don't tell me how to tie you so you can't escape!"

With alarm, Samson said, "If you bind me with new ropes I shall become testosterone-normal."

Delilah excitedly got new ropes and bound Samson. Again she yelled, "The Philistines are here!"

Samson jumped up and the ropes snapped off his arms like threads.

Delilah became anger-endowed, and it wasn't an act. Samson was toying with her and she felt marginalized.

She said, "Samson, how could you be so insensitive to my feelings? How would you feel if I withheld the intimate details of my inner life from you?"

Samson replied, "Okay. Bowstrings and ropes can't hold me. But, if you weave the seven locks of my hair into a tight ball with a loom and put an attractive beret in it, I'll be as physically weak as the feminine species."

Delilah said, "We'll see." She combed Samson's hair into seven locks and wove them into a web with the loom. This felt so pleasurable that Samson went to sleep. When his hair was woven as tightly as an Oriental rug, she called out, "Samson, the Philistines have come!"

Samson woke and shattered the loom and crushed the beret. Still the secret of his strength was not known.

Delilah was frantic. She realized that what she was about to do was a discredit to the sisterhood, but she desired silver more than feminist integrity.

She caused tears to flow down her cheeks and said, "Oh Samson, how can you say that you love

me when you won't share your secrets with me?
Three times you have lied to me. Three times you
have humiliated me and diminished my sense of self.
I'm considering becoming celibate."

Samson was horrified. To sex-deprive one endowed with such great male hormonal reserves
would be libidicide. Samson became desperate, but
still wouldn't have told Delilah his secret if she
hadn't resorted to continual nagging. The combi-
nation of whining and the threat of withholding
conjugal privileges wore down Samson's resolve.

"Delilah, my hair has never been cut because I
have been a Nazarite from birth. If my Nazarite vow
was broken, the Lord, who is the source of my
strength, would desert me and I would become as
weak as a kitten."

Delilah knew she had the truth. She told the
Philistines to come at a prearranged time. "Be sure
to bring the silver," she reminded them.

Before the Philistines arrived, Delilah stroked
Samson's head and he fell asleep on her lap. While
he was sleeping, a barber came and shaved off his

locks. This time when she yelled, "The Philistines are upon you, Samson," he was powerless.

They captured Samson and rendered him optically inconvenienced (after all, they *were* Philistines). They took him to Gaza where he was a guest of the penal system. His new vocation was to grind grain in the mill. However, the Philistines overlooked one important biological fact: Hair eventually grows back.

Several weeks after Samson's capture, the power elite of the Philistines gathered to offer a sacrifice to their god, Dagon. They praised their god, saying, "Dagon has delivered into our hands the Philistine-murdering Samson."

After they had consumed great quantities of the fermented juice of the grape, someone said, "Bring Samson here so that he can entertain us!" So they brought Samson from his suite at the penal institution.

The guards put Samson in the doorway of the huge palace. Everyone waited expectantly to see what kind of dance he would perform. Samson said to the guards, "Let me feel the pillars that support this structure." The guards, supposing that Samson was going to use them for balance, placed his hands on the two pillars.

Samson began to do a can-can with some surprisingly high kicks, much to the delight of the Philistines. The three thousand persons sitting on the roof strained to see this spectacle.

After his dance, Samson took a bow to thunderous applause and shouts of "Encore!" During this break he prayed, "Lord, give me strength one more time so that I may reciprocate for losing my sight." Grasping the two center pillars, Samson strained with all his might against them. Just before the entire palace collapsed, killing everyone, he said a final prayer, "Lord, let me die with the Philistines!" His prayer was answered.

Samson received a burial of honor, being placed in the tomb of his birthfather. Delilah bought herself a salon and became a dresser of hair. For obvious reasons, Nazarites boycotted her establishment.

DAVID AND THE
PERSON OF SIZE

David and Goliath

I Samuel 17

N THE DAYS WHEN
Saul was sovereign of Israel, the persons of Israel and
the persons of Philistia were not very tolerant of one
another. In fact, they were so animosity-inclined toward each other, war broke out between them.

One day, the Israelite and Philistine armies pre-
pared for battle near Elah. The persons of Israel gathered on top of one ridge and the Philistines amassed
on the opposite ridge. A valley separated them and
a river ran through it. Both armies hesitated to fight
in the valley for fear of harming the indigenous

species of plants and insects that flourished there. A Philistine named Goliath, however, tramped into the valley, insensitively ignoring the ecology of this biosystem and its microclimate.

Goliath was size-enhanced. Due to a thyroid condition, he had grown to a height of nine feet and six inches (without sandals). He was an aficionado of heavy metal. His helmet was made of bronze and he wore a coat of mail that weighed over 150 pounds. His shin guards were also made of bronze. His primary weapon was a spear, the head of which weighed nineteen pounds. A massive javelin slung across his shoulders completed his ensemble. He was also gifted in the art of combat, having never been defeated in a contest. In short, Goliath was one intimidating individual.

When he drew within the aural range of the army of Israel, Goliath issued a challenge in a voice so loud it echoed throughout the valley. "Persons of Israel. Why have you come here with an entire army? To settle our differences, we need only two individuals. Choose a person among your ranks and send him or her down to me. We will engage in mortal combat. If your champion wins, then we will be your enslaved persons. If I win, you will become our enslaved persons. What do you say?"

The only sound that came from the Israelite army was that of armor rattling. This was caused by the persons of Israel's knees knocking together. Every member of the Israelite army experienced a courage deficiency. Due to a healthy sense of self-preservation, no person accepted Goliath's challenge. Not even the sovereign, Saul.

Now David happened to come to the front lines the next day to deliver some healthful provisions to his three chronologically gifted siblings, who were soldiers in Saul's army. David, an adolescent preadult, was the youngest of the eight male offspring of Jesse and Nahash.

David heard Goliath's offer, now issued daily, and was disappointed with the persons of Israel's lack of bravery as they responsed with the knocking of knees and silence.

David had difficulty believing that his coequal Israelites would allow this Philistine to verbally abuse the Lord's army. He asked, "What shall be done for the individual who silences this Philistine and takes away the disgrace of Israel? Who does this uncircumcised pagan think he is, defying the army of the living God?"

There was a sharp intake of breath among those who heard David's bold words. David's speech was most insensitive to the Philistine culture; his remark about circumcision bordered on racism. Remembering that he was a preadult, the persons listening attributed his impudence to an adolescent belief in invulnerability. However, one person relayed David's comments to Saul, who immediately asked to meet with David.

When David saw Saul, he proclaimed, "I will go and fight the Philistine Goliath."

Saul said, "Do have a death wish? Have you seen the size of that Philistine? His armor weighs more than you. Besides, you're only a preadult. Goliath has been a warrior longer than you have existed."

David was undaunted: "I am a keeper of sheep for my birthparents. Whenever a lion or tiger or bear coopts a lamb, I rescue the lamb and render the carnivore nonliving."

Saul's attendants cried out, "Lions and tigers and bears, oh my!"

David continued, "This Philistine who has not undergone circumcision, and who has verbally abused God, shall be to me like one of these nonhumyn carnivores. The Lord will save me!"

Saul said, "My, aren't you the empowered one. Go and may the Lord go with you."

Saul dressed David in his personal armor, even though he had misgivings about the blood products that would soon drench it. David strapped on Saul's sword and tried to walk. He took one step and fell over like a balance-impaired person. Like a beetle on its back, David needed assistance to stand up.

David said, "I can't go into battle wearing this heavy armor. I can't even walk."

So David removed the armor, retrieved his shepherd's staff, and walked to a nearby brook. He chose five smooth stones, being careful not to step on the rare moss growing on the rocks. He put the stones in his shepherd's bag and took out his sling. He was ready to meet Goliath, the person of size.

As David walked onto the battlefield, Goliath approached him wearing an expression of surprise. He wondered why this preadult shepherd had wandered onto the battlefield.

Goliath thundered, "Am I a canine companion that the persons of Israel try to defeat me with sticks?"

David said, "I don't understand the metaphor you're employing."

Goliath shouted several expletives involving the name of the Lord, and verbally abused David using the Philistine's gods' names. Having exhausted his negative vocabulary, he shouted down to David, "Come here and I'll feed your flesh to birds and to untamed animal companions."

David responded, "Actually, most birds are not carnivorous. They consume insects."

Goliath jumped up and down as he bellowed, "You Israelite whelp! You would dare to teach me, an educated Philistine, about biology?! I'll make mincemeat of you!"

David said calmly, "Humyn flesh is not normally an ingredient in mincemeat. But getting back to the main point of our verbal exchange . . . you're coming to me with sword and javelin. I'm coming to you in the name of the Lord God!"

Goliath sneered, "Why should I care whose name you are coming in?"

David now became patience-challenged himself. "You have verbally abused the Lord and the persons of Israel. The Lord will strengthen me, thus allowing me to dominate you in battle. I will strike you down and sever your head from your body. Then I will feed *your* flesh and the flesh of the entire Philistine army to the carnivorous birds and to untamed nonhumyn animals. After this is done the entire earth will know that the Lord is God, and that the Lord doesn't need a sword or spear to win a battle."

Goliath said, "That was the longest, most bombastic barrage of verbiage I've ever heard spoken on a battlefield. Why fight me? Just keep talking and I'll kill myself." Goliath meant this facetiously, of course.

David had tolerated enough of Goliath's insensitivity. He ran toward the person of size while removing a stone from his bag. He placed it in the sling and hurled it. Being accuracy-accomplished with a sling, the stone embedded itself into the frontal lobe of Goliath's brain. This had the effect of rendering Goliath unconscious.

Goliath collapsed like a large arboreal companion. David took Goliath's own sword and severed his head, just as he had predicted. David felt a sense of guilt over terminally inconveniencing his opponent, but rationalized his action by reasoning, "This is really a mercy killing. With a severely damaged frontal lobe, Goliath would have had an unacceptably low quality of life."

David's triumph over the Philistine champion had a negative motivational effect on the army of the Philistines. Faced with a "fight or flight" decision, they ran for their lives. Seeing their opponents flee, the male persons of Israel gave chase. But the Philistines, having a head start, outran the Israelites, and preserved their culture. The Israelites returned and did some nontraditional shopping in the deserted Philistine camp.

David took Goliath's head and packed it in salt to preserve it. He asked the scientists of Israel to do medical research on it to determine whether Goliath's thyroid condition was the cause of his aggressive and abusive behavior.

JONAH AND THE
DIFFERENTLY SIZED MAMMAL

Jonah and the Whale

The Book of Jonah

HERE WAS ONCE AN animal rights' activist named Jonah. One day, while Jonah was writing a petition protesting the use of nonhumyn animals in ritual sacrifice, the Lord spoke to him. Actually, the Lord didn't audibly address Jonah, but transposed thoughts into Jonah's mind.

Jonah understood that the Lord wanted him to travel to the great pagan city of Ninevah and suggest they change their moral values and polytheistic belief system. Because Jonah felt that doing this would compromise the Ninevites' self-determination, he decided to flee in the opposite direction.

He booked passage on a ship going to Tarshish. The sailors on the ship were very friendly toward Jonah because he was new in town. In response to their openness, Jonah revealed the reason that he had boarded the vessel.

Suddenly, a tropical depression came over this region of the Mediterranean. The ship was tossed about like a salad. Jonah was sleeping belowdecks, oblivious to the storm.

One of the sailors rousted Jonah saying, "Jonah! Wake up! Communicate with your deity to calm the sea or else we will all be drowned!"

When Jonah came up on deck, he fell down because of the violent listing of the ship on the waves. The sailors, being endowed with primitive decision-making skills, decided to cast lots to determine who was responsible for the storm. Using this ancient method of forecasting, Jonah was singled out as the cause.

Jonah tried to reason with them: "I've already admitted that I am fleeing from my deity. However,

natural events like storms are not caused by super-
natural beings but by a precipitous drop in baro-
metric pressure."

The sailors wouldn't accept Jonah's explanation
and insisted that he was the *prima facie* cause of the
tempestuous weather.

Acceding to peer pressure, Jonah assented: "Then
throw me overboard and see if the sea grows calmer."

They gladly accepted Jonah's offer and tossed him
in the roiling waters. Immediately, the seas ceased
raging, reinforcing the sailors' animistic beliefs.

Jonah, however, was struggling with a difficult
challenge: He couldn't swim. Just as he sank below
the water's surface, a size-enhanced mammal swal-
lowed him whole. Jonah should have been rendered
unconscious by the bilious digestive fluids of the
mammal, but found himself in an air pocket in the
mammal's massive stomach. The air quality was not
high, but at least he could breathe.

For three days and nights, Jonah was a guest in
the stomach of the mammal. This gave him plenty
of time for character evaluation. He decided that, if
he survived this predicament, he would do whatever

the Lord suggested. He expressed this intention nonverbally by dropping to his knees, clasping his hands together, and gazing in an upward direction. Then he buttered up the Lord by singing a song of praise.

The Lord caused the mammal to regurgitate Jonah on dry land, not far from Ninevah. This time, when the Lord invited Jonah to go to Ninevah to suggest a lifestyle change, he sprinted to the city.

Jonah walked through the streets proclaiming, "If this city doesn't engage in a radical reversal of its belief system, in forty days it will become nonexistent."

Jonah was surprised when the Ninevites took these words seriously. The monarch proclaimed a fluids-only fast and coerced everyone into wearing sackcloth to show their seriousness about doing what the Lord asked.

The Ninevites even went so far as to include all their nonhumyn animals in the fast and sackcloth-wearing.

Jonah became outraged that these animal companions were being abused. He said to the Lord,

"It's fine if humyns are into self-deprivation, but to exploit voiceless victims in this way is speciesist! I'm going into the desert to stage a hunger strike! I will not eat until this abuse stops!"

The Lord asked, "Do you believe this extreme response is justified?"

Jonah then projected his anger at the Ninevites onto the Lord. "You always take the side of humyns in these matters, marginalizing animal companions. I knew you would be fooled by the Ninevites' sincerity ploy. They're just trying to save their own skins!"

The Lord tolerated Jonah's tirade in silence. Jonah stomped out into the desert, accidentally stepped on a cactus, and cursed. He sat watching Ninevah, hoping that the Lord would still decide to obliterate it.

As the sun grew hotter, Jonah became dehydrated. The Lord caused a botanical companion to grow beside him. The bush's shade protected Jonah from sunstroke. He was grateful for the shade, but refused to thank the Lord due to negative feelings.

Since Jonah was acting like one, the Lord sent a

worm to keep Jonah company. The worm attacked the root system of the bush and the leaves withered, leaving Jonah exposed to the sun. To punctuate this lesson, the Lord gifted Jonah with a sultry east wind, making the heat unbearable.

Jonah whined like a preadult about the bush, begging to be the recipient of an assisted suicide. The Lord asked, "Do you believe your animosity over the bush is justified?"

Jonah said, "I'm hostile enough to die!"

The Lord decided to reeducate Jonah. "You are so egocentric. You're more concerned about this shade bush than about the well-being of 120,000 Ninevites. Didn't you realize that if I destroyed the city, the animal companions would perish, too? And you call yourself an animal rights' activist."

Jonah replied, "O Lord, I have been self-absorbed. You are absolutely correct. I hadn't considered the consequences of Ninevah's destruction upon voiceless victims. I have decided to change my vocation. I'm becoming a botanical rights' activist. Now, about that bush . . ."